REFLECTIONS
Inspirational Coloring Journal for Teenage Girls

With Original Motivational Quotes

CAMPTYS INSPIRATIONS

Pocket Learner Publishing

Thank you for choosing this coloring journal

If you like this book I'd really appreciate it if you'd leave me a review and have a look at my other books.

REFLECTIONS
Inspirational Coloring Journal for
Teenage Girls

With Original Motivational Quotes

© *Copyright Camptys Inspirations - All rights reserved.*

The content contained in this book may not be reproduced, duplicated or transmitted without direct written permission from the author or publisher. Inspirational quotes – Andrea Campbell's intellectual property

ISBN: 978-1-914997-11-2 (sc)
ISBN: 978-1-914997-12-9 (hc)

Pocket Learner Publishing

A Gift for You

Please join our mailing list to receive periodic updates and materials. You'll also be able to keep abreast of our future publications.

As a thank you please click the following page and download a set of original inspirational quote posters that you can print, frame and position in your favorite space.

https://camptys1.activehosted.com/f/7

Please leave a review

As an independent publisher with a small marketing budget, reviews are very important to us. If you like this material we'd really appreciate it if you could leave us a review on Amazon.

Other Books from the Author

REFLECTIONS
Inspirational Coloring Journal for Women

REFLECTIONS
Inspirational Coloring Journal for Teenage Boys

REFLECTIONS
Inspirational Coloring Journal for Men

REFLECTIONS
Inspirational Coloring Journal for Adults

A range of Activity Books

A selection of Log Books

Inspirational Coloring Book for Teenage Girls

Inspirational Coloring Book for Teenage Boys

Inspirational Coloring Book for Teenage Women

Inspirational Coloring Book for Men

Inspirational Coloring Book for Adults

Inspirational Coloring Book for Boys

Inspirational Coloring Book for Girls

This journal belongs to

_____

*Cows don't coo, and doves don't moo;
in all you are, say and do, be real, and true to you*

REFLECTIONS

Date: _____

What's your interpretation of the quote?

_____
_____
_____
_____

How does the quote apply to your life?

_____
_____
_____
_____
_____
_____
_____
_____
_____
_____
_____

Don't be surprised if your bird doesn't fly if you keep it locked in a cage

REFLECTIONS

Date: _____

What's your interpretation of the quote?

_____
_____
_____
_____

How does the quote apply to your life?

_____
_____
_____
_____
_____
_____
_____
_____
_____
_____
_____

Eagles have no business in chicken squabbles

REFLECTIONS

Date: _____

What's your interpretation of the quote?

How does the quote apply to your life?

*If you can't do it alone, do it together;
and if you can't go together, go it alone*

REFLECTIONS

Date: _____

What's your interpretation of the quote?

How does the quote apply to your life?

*If you don't learn,
you'll be taught*

REFLECTIONS

Date: _____

What's your interpretation of the quote?

_____
_____
_____
_____

How does the quote apply to your life?

_____
_____
_____
_____
_____
_____
_____
_____
_____
_____
_____

*If you have a stone, you can throw it,
but you can choose not to*

REFLECTIONS

Date: _____

What's your interpretation of the quote?

_____
_____
_____
_____
_____

How does the quote apply to your life?

_____
_____
_____
_____
_____
_____
_____
_____
_____
_____
_____
_____

If you wander too far from your source, you're bound to lose your way

REFLECTIONS

Date: _____

What's your interpretation of the quote?

How does the quote apply to your life?

*If you work your gift,
your gift will work for you*

REFLECTIONS

Date: _____

What's your interpretation of the quote?

_____
_____
_____
_____

How does the quote apply to your life?

_____
_____
_____
_____
_____
_____
_____
_____
_____
_____
_____
_____

*If you're a go-getter,
you've got to go get it!*

REFLECTIONS

Date: _____

What's your interpretation of the quote?

_____
_____
_____
_____

How does the quote apply to your life?

_____
_____
_____
_____
_____
_____
_____
_____
_____
_____

If you're not prepared to serve, you're not equipped to lead; leadership is service

REFLECTIONS

Date: _____

What's your interpretation of the quote?

How does the quote apply to your life?

If you're always comfortable and everything is easy, you're not growing

REFLECTIONS

Date: _____

What's your interpretation of the quote?

_____
_____
_____
_____

How does the quote apply to your life?

_____
_____
_____
_____
_____
_____
_____
_____
_____
_____

*Ignorance isn't bliss
when your hair is on fire*

REFLECTIONS

Date: _____

What's your interpretation of the quote?

_____
_____
_____
_____
_____

How does the quote apply to your life?

_____
_____
_____
_____
_____
_____
_____
_____
_____
_____
_____
_____

*In life, it's not about having more;
it's about doing more with what you have*

REFLECTIONS

Date: _____

What's your interpretation of the quote?

How does the quote apply to your life?

*In order to move forward,
sometimes you've got to stand still*

REFLECTIONS

Date: _____

What's your interpretation of the quote?

How does the quote apply to your life?

It is better to run with winners and lose than to run with losers and win

REFLECTIONS

Date: _____

What's your interpretation of the quote?

How does the quote apply to your life?

It is better to walk away limping than to stand firm in the wrong place

REFLECTIONS

Date: _____

What's your interpretation of the quote?

How does the quote apply to your life?

*It's okay to be different
because, in reality, you are*

REFLECTIONS

Date: _____

What's your interpretation of the quote?

_____
_____
_____
_____
_____

How does the quote apply to your life?

_____
_____
_____
_____
_____
_____
_____
_____
_____
_____
_____
_____

Just because you have less doesn't mean that you are worth less

REFLECTIONS

Date: _____

What's your interpretation of the quote?

_____
_____
_____
_____

How does the quote apply to your life?

_____
_____
_____
_____
_____
_____
_____
_____
_____
_____
_____

Just because your hand can reach it doesn't mean that you must pick it

REFLECTIONS

Date: _____

What's your interpretation of the quote?

_____
_____
_____
_____
_____

How does the quote apply to your life?

_____
_____
_____
_____
_____
_____
_____
_____
_____
_____
_____
_____

Learn to ignore the subject but pass the course

REFLECTIONS

Date: _____

What's your interpretation of the quote?

How does the quote apply to your life?

*Life has its ups and downs,
but no one has to be down for you to be up*

REFLECTIONS

Date: _____

What's your interpretation of the quote?

_____
_____
_____
_____

How does the quote apply to your life?

_____
_____
_____
_____
_____
_____
_____
_____
_____
_____
_____

Motivation gets you going, passion keeps you going but it's persistence that gets you there

REFLECTIONS

Date: _____

What's your interpretation of the quote?

_____
_____
_____
_____

How does the quote apply to your life?

_____
_____
_____
_____
_____
_____
_____
_____
_____
_____
_____
_____

No amount of powder can puff away an ugly character

REFLECTIONS

Date: _____

What's your interpretation of the quote?

_____
_____
_____
_____
_____

How does the quote apply to your life?

_____
_____
_____
_____
_____
_____
_____
_____
_____
_____
_____
_____

No matter how expensive the shoes, they still have to touch the ground

REFLECTIONS

Date: _____

What's your interpretation of the quote?

_____
_____
_____
_____
_____

How does the quote apply to your life?

_____
_____
_____
_____
_____
_____
_____
_____
_____
_____
_____
_____

*No one can know everything, do everything or be everything;
don't be afraid to ask for help*

REFLECTIONS

Date: _____

What's your interpretation of the quote?

_____
_____
_____
_____

How does the quote apply to your life?

_____
_____
_____
_____
_____
_____
_____
_____
_____
_____
_____

*No one person can do every single thing,
but every single person can do one thing*

REFLECTIONS

Date: _____

What's your interpretation of the quote?

_____
_____
_____
_____

How does the quote apply to your life?

_____
_____
_____
_____
_____
_____
_____
_____
_____
_____

*Opportunities do not appear
for those who don't prepare*

REFLECTIONS

Date: _____

What's your interpretation of the quote?

_____
_____
_____
_____
_____

How does the quote apply to your life?

_____
_____
_____
_____
_____
_____
_____
_____
_____
_____
_____
_____

*Plan your journey
even if you don't have a ride*

REFLECTIONS

Date: _____

What's your interpretation of the quote?

_____
_____
_____
_____

How does the quote apply to your life?

_____
_____
_____
_____
_____
_____
_____
_____
_____
_____

Sometimes it's harder to do nothing

REFLECTIONS

Date: _____

What's your interpretation of the quote?

How does the quote apply to your life?

Sometimes the best way to speak to someone is to say nothing

REFLECTIONS

Date: _____

What's your interpretation of the quote?

How does the quote apply to your life?

Sow where you don't expect to reap

REFLECTIONS

Date: _____

What's your interpretation of the quote?

_____
_____
_____
_____

How does the quote apply to your life?

_____
_____
_____
_____
_____
_____
_____
_____
_____
_____
_____
_____

Stepping stones may look like stumbling blocks

REFLECTIONS

Date: _____

What's your interpretation of the quote?

_____
_____
_____
_____

How does the quote apply to your life?

_____
_____
_____
_____
_____
_____
_____
_____
_____
_____

Talent without ambition makes for wasted gifting

REFLECTIONS

Date: _____

What's your interpretation of the quote?

How does the quote apply to your life?

The journey of a thousand miles begins in the mind

REFLECTIONS

Date: _____

What's your interpretation of the quote?

_____
_____
_____
_____

How does the quote apply to your life?

_____
_____
_____
_____
_____
_____
_____
_____
_____
_____
_____
_____

The pain is greater when it's later

REFLECTIONS

Date: _____

What's your interpretation of the quote?

_____
_____
_____
_____

How does the quote apply to your life?

_____
_____
_____
_____
_____
_____
_____
_____
_____
_____
_____

*The road to success is dogged with urges to quit.
Don't let the dogs out!*

REFLECTIONS

Date: _____

What's your interpretation of the quote?

_____
_____
_____
_____

How does the quote apply to your life?

_____
_____
_____
_____
_____
_____
_____
_____
_____
_____
_____

Those who have never failed have never tried

REFLECTIONS

Date: _____

What's your interpretation of the quote?

_____
_____
_____
_____

How does the quote apply to your life?

_____
_____
_____
_____
_____
_____
_____
_____
_____
_____
_____

Until you are willing to take the first step, don't think about the next level

REFLECTIONS

Date: _____

What's your interpretation of the quote?

_____
_____
_____
_____

How does the quote apply to your life?

_____
_____
_____
_____
_____
_____
_____
_____
_____
_____

*What we learn gives us a living
but it is what we learn that gives us a life*

REFLECTIONS

Date: _____

What's your interpretation of the quote?

How does the quote apply to your life?

*When the ball falls into the gutter,
it's time to get out of the game*

REFLECTIONS

Date: _____

What's your interpretation of the quote?

_____
_____
_____
_____

How does the quote apply to your life?

_____
_____
_____
_____
_____
_____
_____
_____
_____

*When you know who you are,
it doesn't matter where you are*

REFLECTIONS

Date: _____

What's your interpretation of the quote?

How does the quote apply to your life?

*Who you are determines what you do,
and what you do reveals who you are*

REFLECTIONS

Date: _____

What's your interpretation of the quote?

_____
_____
_____
_____

How does the quote apply to your life?

_____
_____
_____
_____
_____
_____
_____
_____
_____
_____
_____
_____

You can choose to be bitter or choose to be better by changing a letter that you write to yourself

REFLECTIONS

Date: _____

What's your interpretation of the quote?

How does the quote apply to your life?

*You can do a good thing
but it may not be the right thing*

REFLECTIONS

Date: _____

What's your interpretation of the quote?

_____
_____
_____
_____

How does the quote apply to your life?

_____
_____
_____
_____
_____
_____
_____
_____
_____
_____
_____
_____

You can't go places with people who aren't going anywhere

REFLECTIONS

Date: _____

What's your interpretation of the quote?

_____
_____
_____
_____

How does the quote apply to your life?

_____
_____
_____
_____
_____
_____
_____
_____
_____
_____
_____

*You can't lock yourself behind a door
and then complain that no one is reaching out to you*

REFLECTIONS

Date: _____

What's your interpretation of the quote?

How does the quote apply to your life?

*You can't sit on it
and expect it to move*

REFLECTIONS

Date: _____

What's your interpretation of the quote?

How does the quote apply to your life?

*You don't have to flex your muscles in order to win.
Learn to drop it, leave it and let it go.*

REFLECTIONS

Date: _____

What's your interpretation of the quote?

_____
_____
_____
_____

How does the quote apply to your life?

_____
_____
_____
_____
_____
_____
_____
_____
_____
_____

You may be able to achieve anything but there is a season for everything and at some point that season passes.

REFLECTIONS

Date: _____

What's your interpretation of the quote?

_____
_____
_____
_____

How does the quote apply to your life?

_____
_____
_____
_____
_____
_____
_____
_____
_____
_____
_____

*Your circumstances don't define you;
they refine you.*

REFLECTIONS

Date: _____

What's your interpretation of the quote?

How does the quote apply to your life?

Your dream is planted inside of you; don't worry if others can't see it or don't share it. Just don't let them stifle it.

REFLECTIONS

Date: _____

What's your interpretation of the quote?

_____
_____
_____
_____

How does the quote apply to your life?

_____
_____
_____
_____
_____
_____
_____
_____
_____
_____
_____

*Your mentor is not he who advises you;
it's the person whose advice you follow.*

REFLECTIONS

Date: _____

What's your interpretation of the quote?

_____
_____
_____
_____

How does the quote apply to your life?

_____
_____
_____
_____
_____
_____
_____
_____
_____
_____

The following pages are provided for you to document selected passwords, feelings, hopes and dreams as well as your innermost thoughts.

Note also your accomplishments, aspirations and the things for which you are grateful.

Remember to express gratitude for the people who enhance your life.

PASSWORDS

ACCOUNT _____
USERNAME _____
PASSWORD _____

Notes

ACCOUNT: _____
USERNAME _____
PASSWORD _____

Notes

ACCOUNT: _____
AUTHOR: _____
PASSWORD: _____

Notes

ACCOUNT: _____
USERNAME: _____
PASSWORD: _____

Notes

ACCOUNT: _____
USERNAME: _____
PASSWORD: _____

Notes

Date: _____

My Thoughts and Feelings

Date: _____

My Thoughts and Feelings

Date: _____

My Thoughts and Feelings

Date: _____

My Thoughts and Feelings

Date: _____

My Thoughts and Feelings

Date: _____

My Thoughts and Feelings

Date: _____

My Thoughts and Feelings

Date: _____

My Thoughts and Feelings

Date: _____

My Thoughts and Feelings

Date: _____

My Thoughts and Feelings

Date: _____

My Thoughts and Feelings

Date: _____

My Thoughts and Feelings

www.ingramcontent.com/pod-product-compliance
Lightning Source LLC
Chambersburg PA
CBHW060506240426
43661CB00007B/933